ARCHITECTURE:
FORMAL APPROACH

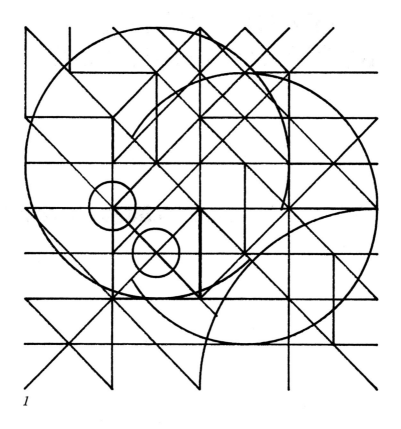

1

ARCHITECTURE: FORMAL APPROACH

Jerzy Wojtowicz and William Fawcett

ACADEMY EDITIONS · LONDON / ST. MARTIN'S PRESS · NEW YORK

720.7
W84a

sf

Published in Great Britain in 1986 by
Academy Editions 7 Holland Street London W8

ISBN 0 85670 885 2

First published 1985

Published in the United States of America in 1986 by
St. Martin's Press 175 Fifth Avenue New York NY 10010

Printed and bound in Great Britain by
The Pindar Group of Companies, Scarborough, North Yorkshire

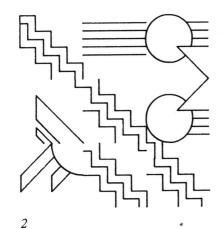

2

Architecture: Formal Approach

Contents:

(front cover) Fragment of computer plotted drawing.
1 (frontispiece) Overlay of six generic elements.
2 Random configuration.
3 Six computer generated "art deco" patterns allow a great number possible of combinations. Only some of them serve as formal ideograms.
4 Dresser. 5 Compact.
6 "Citroen" cabinet.

3

4

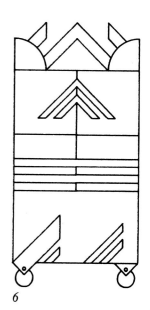

5

6

Opening Movement

The computer has been used in music almost since its inception. Over a quarter-century ago the American composer Hiller used an early Illac computer to compose a piece of music by feeding into it 16th century rules of nodal counterpoint and 20th century ones relating to serialism. "Excluded from the program were all notes that broke the rules, so the computer choose at random from the remaining possibilities. The result was called "The Illac Suite for Strings". In later Hiller works, the notes and intervals were not chosen at random but according to weighted probabilities, e.g. a note was chosen according to implications of the previously chosen note."[2]

Another composer who pioneered the use of computers is Xenakis, at one time a collaborator of Le Corbusier. In some of his compositions he used the theory of games or aleatory procedures to produce music which cannot be predicted before its actual performance.

NB. Computers are used in music not only to aid pre-compositional calculations, to analyse works and to produce systems of notation, but also to produce sound. The invention of Moog's synthesizer presented composers with a spectrum of new sounds and also with astonishing imitative qualities. "The present tendency is to use synthesisers as memory banks, capable of producing any required sounds, memorizing composers' sequence of events, and playing the finished work whenever required."[3]

"It has been said that a person doesn't really understand something until he teaches it to someone else. Actually a person doesn't really understand something until he can teach it to a computer, ie. express it as an algorithm... The attempt to formalise things as algorithms leads to a much deeper understanding than if we try to understand things in the traditional way."
Donald Knuth "Computer science and mathematics" 1975[1]

Structural Rules

A piece of music is a sequence of notes, but we would not expect any random sequence of notes to be recognisable as "music": the sequence is as important as the notes themselves. A musical style is what it is because it defines certain characteristic sequences of notes.

Similarly, an alphabetical language is written by placing letters in a sequence; different languages define different letter sequences. Take the example of English[4]. Here is a random sequence of letters and spaces (ie. it is not specific to English or any language):
XFOML RXKHRJFFJUJ ZLPWCFWKCYJ FFJEYV KCQSGHYD QPAAMKBZAACIBZLHJOD

Now make the frequency of letters correspond to that of English text:
OCRO HLI RGWR NMIELWIS EU LL NBNESEBYA TH EEI ALHENHTTPA OOBTTVA NAH BRL

This lacks much real similarity to English. Next, make the occurrence of adjacent pairs of letters correspond to English:
ON IE ANTSOUTINYS ARE I INCTORE ST BE S DEAMY ACHIN D ILONASIVE TUCOOWE AT TEASONARE FUSO TIZIN ANDY TOBE SEACE CTISBE

The sequence is almost pronounceable as if it was English. Make the occurrence of adjacent triples of letters correspond to English:
IN NO IST LAT WHEY CRACICT FROURE BIRS GROCID PONDENOME OF DEMONSTURES OF THE REPTAGIN IS REGOACTIONA OF CRE

This could hardly be mistaken for any language other than English, even though it is simply a sequence of letters generated at random subject to constraints about letter frequency and adjacency. Clearly these kinds of constraints can represent significant information about the way that English uses the letters of the alphabet.

The exercise can be extended, by regarding English text as a sequence of English words. Take words in accordance with their frequency in English:
REPRESENTING AND SPEEDILY IS AN GOOD APT OR COME CAN DIFFERENT NATURAL HERE HE THE A IN CAME THE OF TO EXPERT GRAY COME TO FURNISHES THE LINE MESSAGE HAD BE THESE

Now take pairs of adjacent words in accordance with their frequency in English:
THE HEAD AND IN FRONTAL ATTACK ON AN ENGLISH WRITER THAT THE CHARACTER OF THIS POINT IS THEREFORE ANOTHER METHOD FOR THE LETTERS THAT THE TIME OF WHO EVER TOLD THE PROBLEM FOR AN UNEXPECTED

This can be read in a fairly naturalistic way, unlike the preceding example; the flow of words is characteristically English.

Music, language – and architecture – exist in structured worlds, whose structure can be represented by precise rules. And within that structure exists art.

"Used in the aesthetic sense, form means that a piece is *organised;* ie. that it consists of elements functioning like those of a living *organism.* Without organisation music would be an amorphous mass, as unintelligible as an essay without punctuation, or as disconnected as a conversation which leans purposelessly from one subject to another. The chief requirements for the creation of a comprehensible form are *logic* and *coherence."* **Arnold Schoenberg** *Fundamentals of Musical Composition,* **1967**[5]

Teaching, Knowledge and Design Procedures

Design Crit...

Tutor: Hi! What are you working on?

Student: On elevation and roof treatment.

Tutor: By "treatment" do you mean curing moisture or some other sickness?

Student: Oh, yes!

Tutor: Which?

Student: My problem has nothing to do with waterproofing, it is a formal question.

Tutor: Formal questions are rather tricky. Could you please restate it?

Student: How to express the entry in relation to the facade of my project?

Tutor: By "express", do you mean represent?

Student: I mean to draw, to design.

Tutor: Shall we look at your drawings?

Student: Here comes the last one, no. 213.

Tutor: Do you like it?

Student: It stinks, I mean I am not happy with it at all.

Tutor: I see... Would you like to examine how entry conditions were resolved by your honourable predecessors?

Student: OK. While I am not much into ancestor worship it might save me going through the glossies.

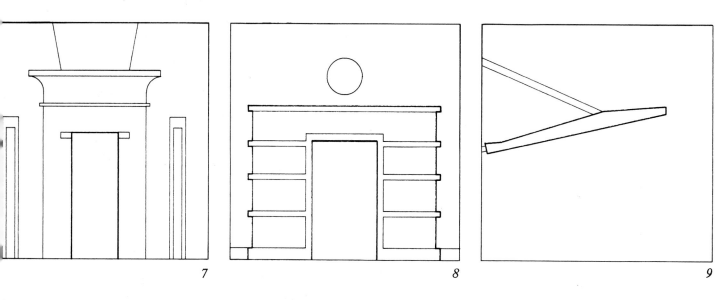

7

8

9

10

*Computer plotted entries from
"data base of precedents".
7 Great Pylon, Temple of Horus,
Edfu, 200 BC.
8 Karl Marx Hof, Vienna, Karl
Ehn, 1927.
9 and 10 Villa Stein, Garches,
Le Corbusier, 1927.*

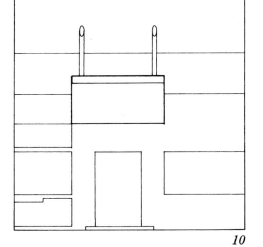

10

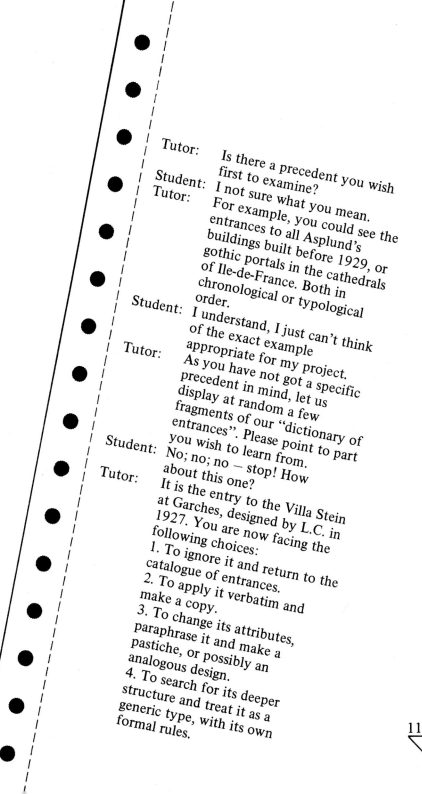

Tutor: Is there a precedent you wish first to examine?

Student: I not sure what you mean.

Tutor: For example, you could see the entrances to all Asplund's buildings built before 1929, or gothic portals in the cathedrals of Ile-de-France. Both in chronological or typological order.

Student: I understand, I just can't think of the exact example appropriate for my project.

Tutor: As you have not got a specific precedent in mind, let us display at random a few fragments of our "dictionary of entrances". Please point to part you wish to learn from.

Student: No; no; no — stop! How about this one?

Tutor: It is the entry to the Villa Stein at Garches, designed by L.C. in 1927. You are now facing the following choices:
1. To ignore it and return to the catalogue of entrances.
2. To apply it verbatim and make a copy.
3. To change its attributes, paraphrase it and make a pastiche, or possibly an analogous design.
4. To search for its deeper structure and treat it as a generic type, with its own formal rules.

11

Knowledge-based Expert Systems

In the 1960's there was a strong impetus to bring to architecture a substantial input of theory. The "design methods" movement followed the precedent of natural science: its ideal was to use then-new computers to discover a compact, universal set of precise laws that would explain scientifically the empirical facts of architecture. It failed. Despite laws of geometry and constraints of function, the products of design – architectural forms – are a matter of choice, not necessity. If architectural theory cannot be modelled as a natural science, can it be as artificial intelligence?

One of artificial intelligence's key ideas is that people do not rely on super-high-speed calculation to solve problems, but on knowledge: we **know** the past tense of "he goes", the product of 6 times 8, the behaviour of an umbrella in a typhoon. To model human intellectual abilities, knowledge-intensive representations are needed. AI models use computers very differently from the natural sciences. Instead of programs consisting of concise equations which number-crunch masses of data, the computer becomes a vast storehouse of **knowledge**, held in small, independent pieces which can be incrementally modified or added to. In operation the computer follows a path (at very high speed, of course) around this storehouse, picking things out, following a scent, with one item leading to another, until a conclusion is reached. Pattern-matching is the guiding principle of operation: if you have to join two components, check the materials; if they're steel, consider welding; for welding check the steel thickness; is the welding insitu or off-site; if welding if off-site, can the components be moved; for on-site fabrication, what about tolerances; what about tolerances of subcomponents fixed to the components in question; and so on.

The distinction, so important in traditional scientific theories, between **program** and **data** falls away, replaced by **knowledge** that can include facts and rules indiscriminately.

The term "expert system" is used to describe knowledge-based computer software that can perform tasks requiring a degree of expertise in humans. Usually they are consultation programs – a user gets advice from the system as he would when consulting a human expert. Successful expert systems have been constructed for medical diagnosis, mineral prospecting, computer configuration, molecular analysis, taxation advice, chess-playing. Why not architecture?

The most tantalising precedent is an expert system called R1 for configuring mini-computers. A mini-computer system is specified by selecting items from a very long catalogue of options; there are so many permutations that each system is effectively unique. The configuration task is to design a functioning 3-dimensional layout within standard cabinets for a given component list. It was a task performed by design engineers, using experience and intuition in the same way as all designers do. They were asked what they knew about the task they performed, and described about 200 rules. An expert system was built using them, but it kept failing. Whenever it failed the engineers were asked why, and they were able to point out the factors that caused failures. In this way the expert system was built up to 700 rules, when it could perform pretty much as well as the engineers. The engineers did have knowledge which they held in an inexplicit, intuitive way, but the knowledge was capable of being made explicit and precise.

Student: I cannot decide on the empty stomach. As you said, formal questions are rather tacky... Perhaps after lunch, say 2.30?

The above exchange is not particularly unusual and could have taken place in any School of Architecture. What is remarkable about this conversation is that today the same crit of the student's project might have been given by a computer-based design expert system.

The computer-man dialogue, as well as the scope of this monograph, is limited to the formal aspects of architectural design. The other Vitruvian principles, that is Firmitas and Utilitas, are absent here, so is the question of meaning. The boundry of Design Knowledge is one of form and its generating structures, both essential to the making of architecture.

"The art of architectural production," observed Jorge Silvetti, "is inevitably an art of transformation of knowledge."[7] This could well serve as the definition of design education. However, the difference between teaching and making architecture is in the degree to which conventions are made intelligible. Perhaps a similar variance exists between the teaching of music and its performance. Yet the conventions of method and model which are so clear in music are far more elusive in contemporary architecture. Like in the conservatory, so in a design school we need explicit rules of composition in order to write even a simple design etude.

13

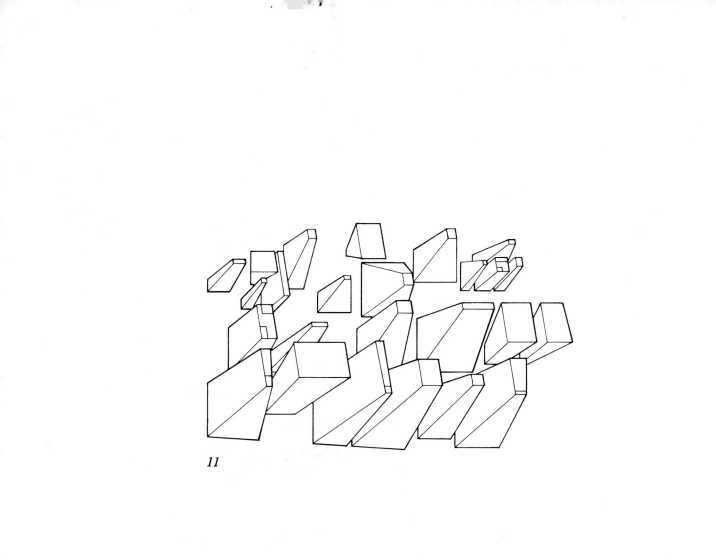

11

12

Reading architecture
11 Six reducing and fourteen
amplifying light prisms read from
the south facade of Le Corbusier's
Chapel of Notre-Dame-du-Haut,
Ronchamp, 1954.
12 Twenty Ronchamp windows
arranged according to the intensity
of light transmitted.

Without conventions and form we would not be able to read, study and to interpret the masterpieces marking the ascent of our culture. Without them we cannot perform and write music or make architecture. Viollet le Duc put it well: "The first condition of design is to know what we have to do; to know what we have to do, is to have an idea; to express this idea we must have principles and form; that is grammar and language". [8]

For design, literacy has to do with the ability to read and write architecture. NB The skill of reading is more than just appreciating and intuitively recognising the formal quality of the object. Reading architecture has to do with the process of parsing or resolving the elements and parts of a building and describing them grammatically. Reading architecture is a prerequisite to writing, constructing or composing it.

Architecture can be discussed either as a natural or as a formal language. Natural languages cannot be invented, but have to evolve as a means of communication between people. Yet even natural language is believed to be a super-complicated collection of formal languages and conventions. Learning architecture can be understood as the acquisition of a formal design language, its generating rules or grammar.

Many architects find the notion of formal design knowledge too limiting and too untried to be useful. Yet most of design is very certain indeed, since it is dealing with the generation or transformation of objects. Architectural form is exact and precise because it is expressed with geometry. Geometry is essential in both reading and generating design; to use Khan's words, "Geometry is the mother of invention". [9]

15

Imitation

"In the field of Chinese calligraphy, as in other fields of art, imitation of the work of old masters is always the key to success. Students of calligraphy should undergo three stages of imitation study: 1. Imitation by means of writing over coloured strokes; 2. Imitation by means of writing on a superimposed sheet of paper; 3. Imitation by means of copying."[10]

The first stage, intended for primary students, is a prerequisite to the latter two. The student has to practice writing over printed red characters with black ink brush strokes until a perfect match with the master pattern is achieved. A page from a typical exercise book illustrates this imitation method.

The second step involves tracing the printed master characters on a superimposed sheet of paper. As traditional rice paper is transluscent and not transparent, the process of imitation is slightly less direct.

The third level involves copying when the object of imitation is placed in front of the student. The model is often an ink-rubbing from an ancient inscription, making imitation more difficult.

The ultimate criterion of competence in Chinese calligraphy is known as pei-lin, or "imitation from memory".

The notion of imitation is present in western art, but is less exact and also less limiting. "I am not only very much disposed to maintain the absolute necessity of imitation in the first stages of art; but I am of the opinion that the study of other masters, which I here call imitation, may be extended throughout our whole lives,"[11] states the XVIII century English academician, Sir Joshua Reynolds.

Fragments of his Discourses on Art elegantly illustrate both the importance and limits of imitative methods. "I am persuaded that by imitation only, variety and even originality of invention is produced... Invention is one of the great marks of genius, but if we consult experience, we shall find that it is by being conversant with the inventions of others that we learn to invent, as by reading the thought of others we learn to think... A mind enriched by an assemblage of all the treasures of ancient and modern art will be more elevated and fruitful in resources in proportion to the number of ideas which have been carefully collected and thoroughly digested."[12]

Reynolds makes a very clear distinction between copying and imitation: "When I speak of the habitual imitation and continued study of masters, it is not to be understood that I advise any endeavour to copy the exact peculiar colour and complexion of another man's mind; the success of such an attempt must always be like his, who imitates exactly the air, manner, and gestures, of him whom he admires. His model may be excellent but the copy will be ridiculous."[13]

The importance of the creative aspect of imitation is well understood by Reynolds. "The artist should enter into competition with his original, and endeavour to improve what he is appropriating in his own work. Such imitation is so far from having anything in it of the servility of plagiarism, that it is a perpetual exercise of the mind, a continual invention."[14]

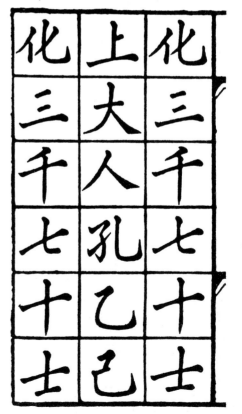

"In general, the less you make servile copies, the more quickly you will progress in understanding the mechanism of composition."
Durand, *Partie graphique*, 1821[15]

13 Page from Chinese calligraphy pattern book.

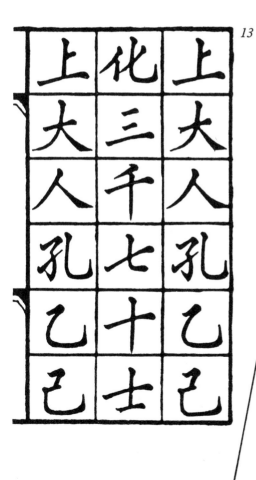

13

Teaching and making architecture cannot be based on the black box principle, where every new design problem triggers an original, new solution.

The creative act of design is occasionally associated with "innovation", where new objects or techniques are created to solve a given problem. This aspect of design could be compared to the fundamental research needed to develop the completely new product. The other and often understated aspect of design could be compared to product development, where the notion of precedent is recognised. Here modification, assessment, editing, choice and consultation with archives of collective memory are among the important design procedures.

Designers solve formal problems by establishing constraints. Their rules or constraints are not always explicit or rational, but are frequently based on the exploration of alternative solutions. Design constraints on form are often implicit, and operate within the limits of a personal design grammar and vocabulary.

Design can be understood as a knowledge-based system of conventions. Since it has to do with information and image processing, design can also be understood as vast database or expert system with knowledge accessible on a need-to-know basis.

Accepting the need for knowledge-based architectural design one can turn to the field of Artificial Intelligence for more specific procedures and problem-solving structures. Two of these procedures are of particular importance to design:

1. Generate and test, where conclusions are generated and than evaluated for correctness.

2. Constrained generation, where only a subset of possible solutions are examined.

17

Explicit "production rules"
existed in diverse classical cultures.
14 Plate of the orders from a
typical handbook of classical
architecture.

15 Plate from Architectural Design
and Construction Manual of the
Sung Dynasty.

14

15

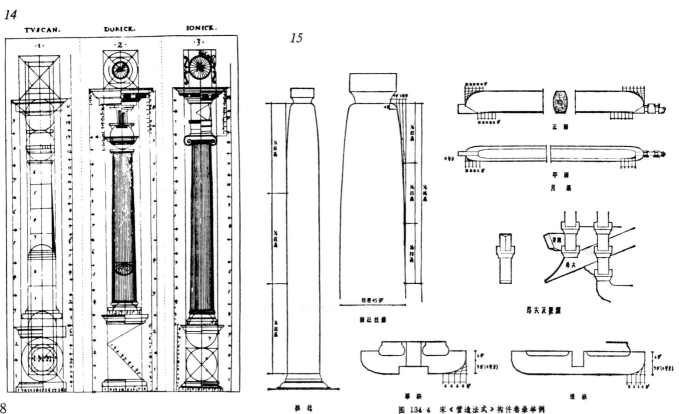

Lutyens describes using the Doric order from Sammichele: "You cannot copy: you find if you do you are caught, a mess remains. It means hard labour, hard thinking, over every line in all three dimensions and in every joint, and no stone can be allowed to slide. If you take it this way, the Order belongs to you, and every stroke, being mentally handled, must become endowed with such poetry and artistry as God has given you. You alter one feature (which you have to, always), then every other feature has to sympathise and undergo some care and invention. Therefore it is no mean game, nor is it a game you can play lightheartedly."

From a letter written in 1911[16]

In order to generate solutions both procedures need the application of production rules. The rules are explicit but not static, their values can be assigned, manipulated and selectively applied. The rules represent knowledge. Architecture has to do with the exercise of explicit artistic decision, precise judgment and rules.

Many would argue that expert systems in architecture are of particular interest to those who want to automate and regulate design procedures. The dangers and limits of such a prospect are evident. Equally obvious are the advantages; those who are less skilled, or students of the subject, will in the end benefit the most. The broader opportunities were recognised a decade ago by Negroponte: "The industrial revolution brought sameness through repetition and amortization through duplication. In contrast, information technologies — soft machines — afford the opportunity for custom made, personalised artifacts."[17]

Today there is a need for rule based, additive and explicit models of design knowledge, if designed artifacts are to mark and not to litter the ascent of man. Today concepts like analogy, typology or memory need to be made precise enough to be computable. **Only then computers will be to architecture, what instruments are to music.**

Generate-and-Test vs. Constrained Generation

One way of getting at interesting patterns of objects is to generate random patterns and then select the interesting ones, or even to generate exhaustively all possible patterns and again make a selection. Only on a small scale is exhaustive enumeration possible.

The library at Aalto's Saynatsalo Town Hall has a long composite window made up of ten bays, each bay of five lights. There are tall lights and short ones. So Aalto's window is a sequence of bays, and each bay is a sequence of tall and short lights. There are thirty-two possible bay designs; ▽Aalto used four.

The window has ten bays. If any of the 32 bay designs could be used in any bay, there would be approximately 1 125 900 000 000 000 alternative elevations. If only Aalto's four bay designs were used there would be 1 048 576 possible elevations. Quite obviously these cannot be listed exhaustively; and the likelihood of hitting on a good design by random generation in a reasonable length of time is slight. Generate-and-test is not viable.

The alternative is to identify the structure of good sequences, and to use it to generate only good sequences. Let us apply this principle first to the design of the bay. Consider two constraints:
1. a bay cannot have one tall and four short lights,
2. the tall lights in a bay must be grouped together.

This allows Aalto's four bay designs, and also seven others, extending the language beyond the built examples used at Saynatsalo. All eleven bays are ⃝marked in the drawing.

What about the sequence of bays? Suppose there is the constraint:
3. all tall lights must be grouped together in two zones.

Aalto's design conforms to this; we can generate many designs that do so as well:

These have fewer tall lights than Aalto's design; let us add the constraint:
4. there are 29 short lights and 21 tall lights.

This reduces the number of possible designs for the composite window, but there are still many:

We could impose further constraints, relating for example to the symmetry or asymmetry of the elevation, or to the adjacency of different bays, and so on. Whatever constraints we impose, we can generate corresponding designs.

Aalto produced only one design. If we copy it, we can only repeat and repeat his one design. By identifying and making explicit the structure that differentiates his design from a random pattern, we can do more than copy — we can create new designs in Aalto's language.

In all figures the symbol ▽ indicates a design actually used by the architect.

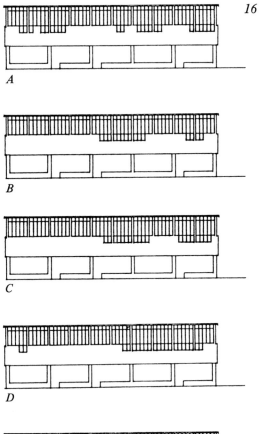

16

A

B

C

D

E

16 Composite windows. Design A obeys none of the rules. Designs B and C obey rules 1, 2 and 3. Designs D and E obey rules 1, 2, 3, and 4.

16F Aalto's design for the library elevation, Saynatsalo Town Hall.

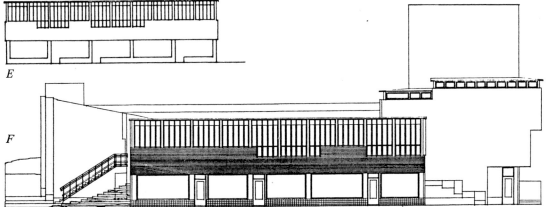

F

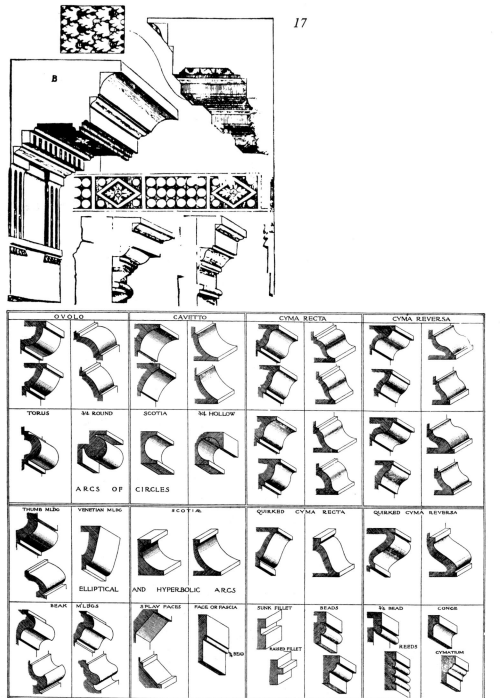

Memory, Typology and CAD

In architecture, the presence of rule-based design expert systems is not new. From the exact classical orders and Durand's compositions, to the less precise pastiches of L.C. by NY 5, or Mies by his IIT students, rule-based or precedent-based formal conventions were used by architects with various degrees of explicitness.

The publication of the early architectural treatieses, by Serlio, Palladio and Vignola, provided generations of designers with models and canons for classical architectural forms. Those Renaissance treatises were influenced by the text of Vitruvius, (which survived with no illustrations), and contained numerous "measured drawings" of ancient architectural details and buildings. Because of the above disclosures, the architect's memory has been extended. Even those who never visited Rome to learn from it at first hand, were soon able to read and write classical architecture.

Over time, the notion of architectural memory became equated with the recognition of models and precedents in the process of design of new architecture.

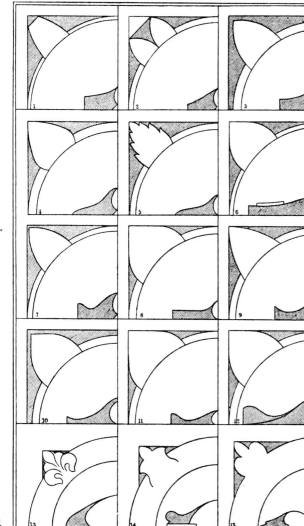

Typology vs Classification

"*Typology stands for system of groupings (types), which aid demonstration or investigation by establishing a* **limited relationship** *among phenomena.*"[18]*As a method it can be well used for the study of variables, as the type need deal with only one attribute in question. The adjacent illustration from* The Stones of Venice[19]*makes an instructive example: Ruskin employed here the typological method to examine a single aspect of column bases – that of spurs. To understand the deeper structure he drew quadrants of fifteen bases within squares of equal size, irrespective of the real dimensions of the examined objects. His argument about the inferiority of "rude" French bases (the bottom three) vs. the remainder (Italian of course) is of lesser interest today than the rigour of his typological analysis. Typology is often engaged by archaeology, art history or anthropology in the examination of the particular aspects of objects in question. Classification in turn can be seen as a method limited only to the problem of order.*

Consider the adjacent collection of 22 buttons. The attempt to classify such a random collection according t *natural class or to order it by degree of resemblance, is less relevant than a typological examination. The prevailing type (boxed-in) is exemplifie* d *by nine buttons, each differen* t *in terms of size, material, colour, weight, price, place of origin, or garment style it is destined for. The sentence: "Four identical holes are positioned symetrically on tw* o *perpendicular diameters of a round disk" – is an exhaustiv* e *description of the nine butto* r *typological structure. It migh* t *also well serve as generating rule for making hundreds upo* n *hundreds of different looking buttons, all linked by the common type.*

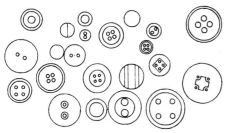

20

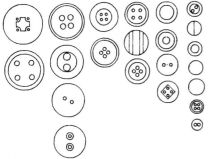

21

22

19 Plans of column bases,
quadrants, and spurs, from John
Ruskin's Stones of Venice, 1851.
20 Random collection of buttons.
21 Buttons classified by size.
22 Prevailing button type boxed-
in.

This notion was first threatened by the eclectic abuses of historical styles in "archaeological" reconstructions of the Ecole des Beaux Arts, and was firmly terminated by the anti-historical posture of the Modern Movement.

The Modern Movement rejected also the idea of architecture openly structured on typology, by replacing the notion of type with the prototype.[20] The concept of typology is rooted in natural science and the rationalist thought of XVII century. The precise definition of an architectural type was given by Quatremere de Quincy in his *Dictionnaire de l'Architecture*:

"The word 'type', does not present so much an image of something to be copied or exactly imitated, as the idea of an element which should itself serve as a rule for the model... 'the model' understood as a part of the practical execution of art is an object which should be imitated for what it is; the type on the other hand is something in relation to which different people may concive works of art having no obvious resemblance to each other. All is exact and defined in 'the model'; in the type everything is more or less vague. Imitation of types therefore has nothing about it which defies the operation of sentiment and intelligence."[21]

In architecture, as in other rational disciplines, the concept of "type" becomes an abstraction, a principle, a starting point. "The type can be also thought of as a frame within which change operates... The architect can extrapolate from the type, change its use, distort the type by means of transformation of scale, or overlap different types to product new ones," observed Rafael Moneo.[22]

Top-down and bottom-up

A completed design is the end-product of a process. What does the process start with? And how does it move from the starting point to the actual design?

Suppose it starts with a vocabulary of well-defined physical components. The process of design involves selecting components from the vocabulary (the same component may be selected a number of times), placing the first one, and adding the others successively. Louis Kahn's Richards Medical Laboratories can be interpreted as the outcome of such a process. The vocabulary of components comprises a square laboratory tower, a main core block, and a secondary core block.

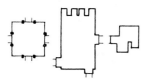

It is natural to place the main core first. The laboratory towers can be added in many ways; secondary towers terminate extended groups of towers. Just a few possible designs are shown; the difference between linear and branching designs is notable. ▽ Kahn's design in marked.

23

A different starting point for the design process is an abstract geometrical or topological concept, which is progressively elaborated until it is finally transformed into the disposition of a physical building. Le Corbusier's Villa Savoye can be interpreted in this way. It begins with a square, which is then subdivided by a square grid. The enclosing square is extended along one axis. The two floors can now be considered separately. On the ground floor some spatial enclosure and circulation elements are added; similarly on the first floor. Columns are located — some of the intersections of the square grid, some displaced along grid-lines, and some omitted on the first floor. Further partitions and openings have to be added to complete the plan.

Kahn's building is an example of the "bottom-up" approach, and Le Corbusier's the "top-down" approach. One starts with physical components (the "bottom" of a national hierarchy of design concepts) and additively creates a design out of them; the other starts with an abstract concept (the "top" of the notional hierarchy) and progressively transforms it into physical reality.

In all figures the symbol ▽ indicates a design actually used by the architect.

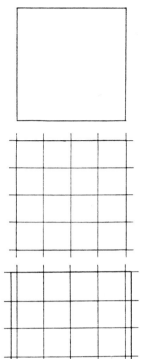

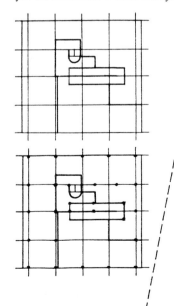

23 "Bottom-up" designs made
from the components of Kahn's
Richards Medical Laboratory
building.
24 "Top-down" design sequence
for Le Corbusier's Villa Savoye.

The typological mechanism is more than a method of analytical observation, classification and comparison. It is the very possibility of producing objects. The decomposition and analytical fragementation of architectural objects results in the creation of a formal data-base or catalogue of typological elements; it is not an end in itself, but a step in the design process.

One gathers knowledge through a process of knowledge acquisition. Creative designers accumulate a rich, personal database of images, formal information and precedents, and subject it to strict though not always obvious rules and application procedures. Le Corbusier, for example assigned great importance to the process of developing an artistic vocabulary, which he named "recherches patientes". Initially he adopted the forms of ordinary objects like bottles, musical instruments or industrial products, later he added fragments of his own projects as models and types. He called them "objets types". References often entered his personal design data base via painting, and included "types de reaction poethique", built out of fragments of organic forms like shells, nudes, etc. While artists rearly make the creative procedure so explicit as Le Corbusier, in the learning environment and when dealing with collective design knowledge, rules have to be made transparent for the user's examination.

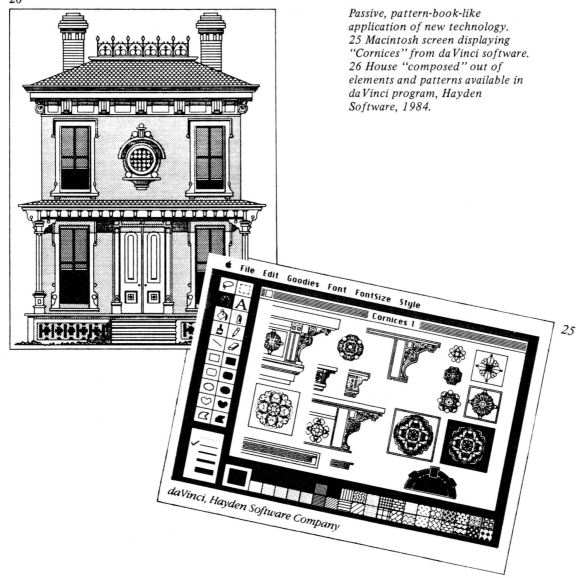

Passive, pattern-book-like
application of new technology.
25 Macintosh screen displaying
"Cornices" from daVinci software.
26 House "composed" out of
elements and patterns available in
daVinci program, Hayden
Software, 1984.

25

daVinci, Hayden Software Company

In current architectural culture the notion of analogy or reference to precedent are part of the loose artistic license. Similarly, the encyclopaedist's concept of typology and the anthropologist's notion of collective memory are readmitted to architecture. Yet they all remain far from any explicit method, and are used mostly as dialectic weapons or as elegant but obscure artistic tools of the avant guard. Rossi's position is case in point: "Now I seem to see all the things I have observed arranged like a tools in a neat row, or a catalogue, or a dictionary. But this catalogue, lying somewhere between imagination and memory, is not neutral; it reappears in several objects and constitutes their deformation and in some way, their evolution".[23]

Today, Memory and Typology in Architecture gain extraordinary significance and dimension with the growing acceptance of Computer Aided Design (CAD). The Impact of this new tool can only be compared to the introduction of printing and engraving in the Renaissance, which enabled the dissimination of architectural thought via illustrated records of precedents, types and rules of antiquity. With CAD feedback through the storage, evaluation and manipulation of formal constructs, from the recent and distant past; the instant interaction and access of many designers to a common but continually upgraded graphic data base, become possible.

Will Computer Aided Design make architects use precedents while searching for invention? Will it extend the limits of their memory? Will it bring about a new architecture of the silicon age?

Vocabulary and Language

Language consists of arrangements of the words in a vocabulary, and new sentences are made by arranging the vocabulary in new ways. Similarly, a design is an arrangement of elements, and new designs can be created by arranging given elements in a new way.

Designs can also be described by the values given to a number of attributes, and new designs created by giving new values. In the monastery of La Tourette, Le Corbusier designed a number of different rooflights – an imaginative tour-de-force:

Suppose these rooflights are simplified to a three-dimensional form between two planes; then each can be described by four attributes:
1. What is the cross-section of the light?
2. Does the light taper in or out?
3. Are the two planes parallel?
4. Is the axis of the light perpendicular to one of the planes?

Le Corbusier's lights can be represented by the values given to these attributes.

By giving new values to these attributes new rooflights can readily be created.

If new attributes are introduced the variety of rooflights can be further increased.
5. does the rooflight branch?
6. does the rooflight twist?

The new possibilities can be indicated by two examples.

Invention becomes easy. Is it surprising that architects were able to go on designing classical buildings for hundreds of years without exhausting the language?

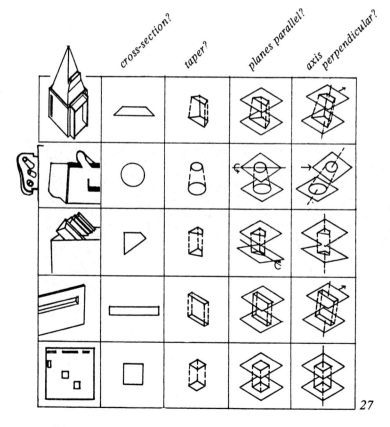

27 Five existing rooflights in Le Corbusier's La Tourette analysed according to four attributes.
28 Twelve possible rooflight types generated from a square cross-section.
29 Model of La Tourette, Le Corbusier, 1957.

"It seems to me impossible to accept the view that linguistic behaviour is a matter of habit... Ordinary linguistic behaviour characteristically involves innovation, formation of new sentences and new patterns in accordance with rules of great abstractness and intricacy. This is true both of the speaker, who constructs new utterances appropriate to the occasion, and of the hearer who must analyse and interpret these novel structures... The new utterances that are produced and interpreted are 'similar' to those that constitute the past experience of the speaker and hearer only in that they are determined, in their form and interpretation, by the same system of abstract underlying rules."

Noam Chomsky, 1965[24]

Objects and Rules

Let us take it that a design has two aspects: first, a number of components, and secondly, a relationship between the components. Or, a design has **objects** and **rules**.

The objects we see; rules are rather intangible, since they do not have a separate physical existence in the design. Nevertheless it is the rules that distinguish a random pattern of objects from a significant design. How can we use objects and rules to express the structure of a design, in such a way that new designs can be created?

Suppose we concentrate on the objects. The objects out of which a design is made can be enumerated, and so can characteristic examples of the ways the objects are combined. This might be called a "catalogue" approach. When studying finished designs, which are the primary resource for acquiring architectural knowledge, we find that only the complete design exists, so we have to extract the catalogue of objects by "decomposing" the design; and also, we only see one way of combining the objects, in the design itself, so alternative combinations are a matter of inference or speculation.

Taking as an example Stirling & Gowan's Leicester Engineering tower, the component objects can readily be extracted and catalogued.

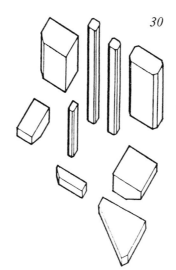

30

30 The nine component objects out of which the tower at Stirling & Gowan's Leicester Engineering Building is composed.
31 Twelve examples from a catalogue of compositions using the objects in the Leicester Engineering tower, starting with the original (top left), and moving to designs that are increasingly "unlike" the original (bottom right).
32 Four shape rules to define explicitly some characteristics of Stirling & Gowan's composition.

There are many ways of re-combining these objects, some of which seem to echo the structure of the original design, others manifestly not. We can build up a catalogue of "good" designs; the more designs we get in the catalogue the more fully we indicate the principles of composition, and the easier it should be to create new compositions.

In the catalogue approach, the rules of composition are implicit. Intelligence is assumed in the user of the catalogue, who has to internalise the principles implicit in the catalogued examples. Alternatively we can make the rules explicit; the following rules

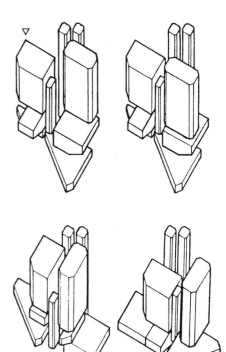

correspond to the catalogue of good compositions.

When given the objects and also explicit rules of combination the generation of new designs is more straightforward, and a catalogue of good designs more easily constructed. But this catalogue of compositions is actually redundant – if we are given the objects and rules, the entire range of possible compositions is implicitly specified, and can be generated quite mechanically when required.

This is interesting: a purely object-based catalogue approach relies on implicit rules; when rules become ex-plicit, objects are implied and no longer need to be catalogued. This is true of compositions; is it true for the component objects also? Rules of combination necessarily include a description of the objects being combined, and these descriptions are merely repeated in an object catalogue. A wholly rule-based approach can thus include all information presented in an object-based catalogues, and add the explicit definition of rules that are implicit (but essential) in the object-based method. Objects can be generated at will, both components and compositions.

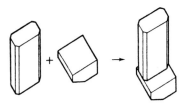

Higher blocks must be placed above lower ones

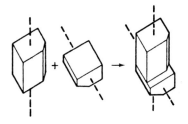

Blocks with perpendicular axes can be stacked

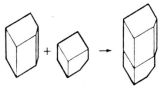

Blocks with the same number of faces can touch

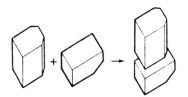

Blocks with a different number of faces must be separated

32

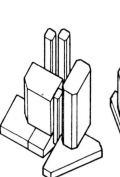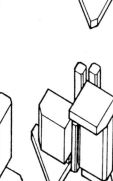

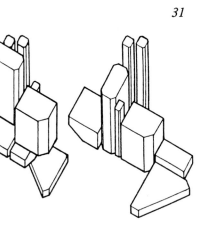

31

33

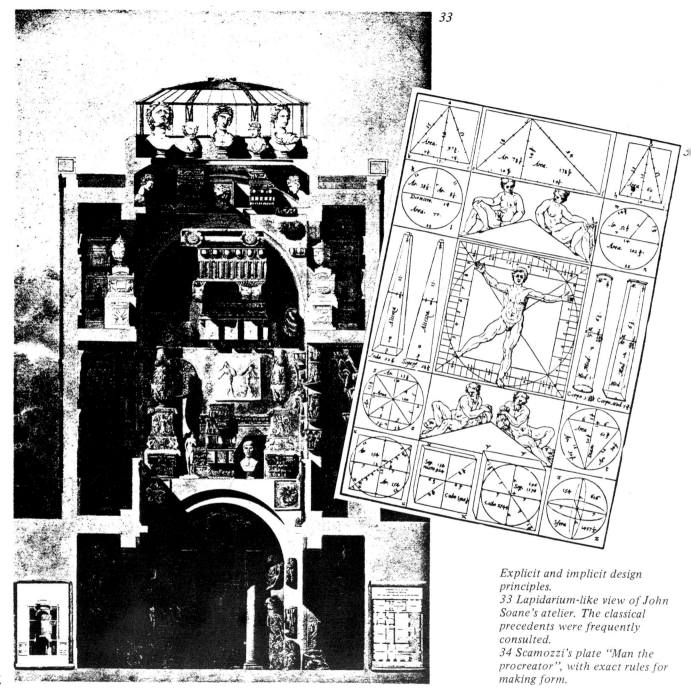

Explicit and implicit design principles.

33 Lapidarium-like view of John Soane's atelier. The classical precedents were frequently consulted.

34 Scamozzi's plate "Man the procreator", with exact rules for making form.

"Many architects say that rules and method are shackles of genius. Far from sharing that opinion, we think on the contrary that they facilitate its development and assure its progress; besides, reason can do without genius, whereas genius cannot avoid error unless it is led and enlightened by reason."

Durand, *Precis* (vol.2), 1817[25]

Achtung: Canons!

In 1984/85 "Topics in Architecture"[26] moved away from the case study method, concerned with the descriptive examination of contemporary architecture, to the search for principles of design. The underlying objective is to make architectural knowledge and its teaching explicit and to facilitate the intellectual appropriation of **formal** precedents in design.

Two models for representing formal principles of design were selected and subjected to closer scrutiny. One following Durand and the other based on Shape Grammars. Both are open-ended systems of design, whose results are constrained by canons or rules established a priori. The rules are more explicit in Shape Grammars and less so in Durand, who relies on the authority of a particular architectural style. Both methodologies are concerned solely with **formal** aspects of architectural design.

35

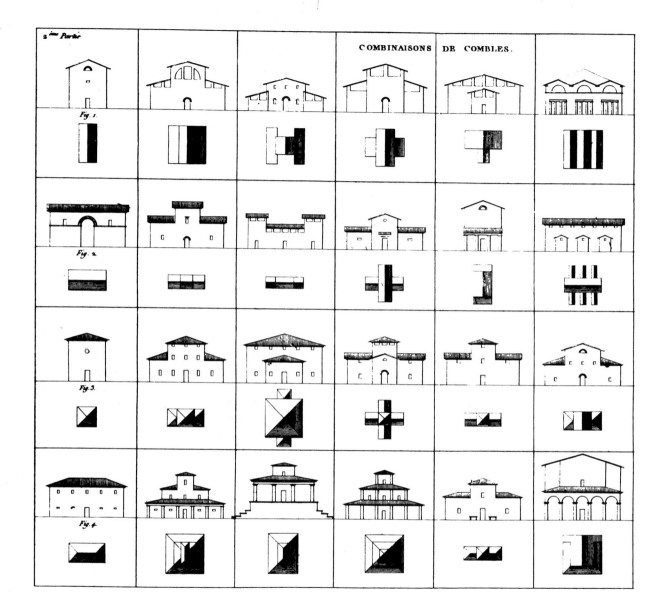

35 Combinations of hipped roofs,
Durand, 1802. The four generic
types are organised in order of
increasing complexity.

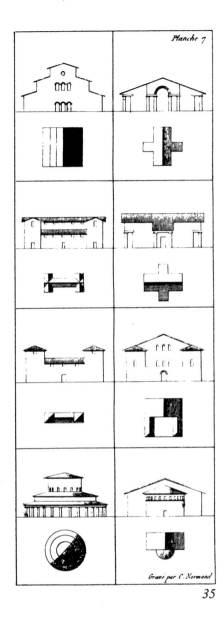

Planche 7

Gravé par C. Normand

35

1. Durand's Method.

"Not the least reason for the popularity of Durand's book lay in its value as a pattern book," observes Branham.[27] Benevolo reduces Durand method to "a sort of theory of combination, an exercise in juxtaposing the given elements in every possible way..."[28] Other contemporary critics link the historical importance of Durand's method to the question of normative typology. According to Frampton, Durand, "the first tutor in Architecture at the Ecole Polytechnique, sought to establish a universal building methodology, an architectural counterpart to the Napoleonic Code, by which economic and appropriate structures could be created through the modular permutation of fixed plan types and alternative elevations."[29] To Watkin, Durand "represents the culumination of the drier aspects of this somewhat puritanical rationalism".[30]

Durand's system of architectural notation is of course much more elegant and important than that. The opening sentence in the introduction to his *Precis des Lecons d'Architecture* reads, **"L'Architecture est l'art de composer et d'executer** tous les edefices publics et particuliers."[31] Today with amusement we recognise that in French the two verbs "composer" and "executer" can also apply to the **composition** and **performance** of music — architecture is the art of composing and performing all buildings both public and private. Their presence and usage in architecture is not central to Durand's argument, it is so obvious and natural that is left undefined.

37

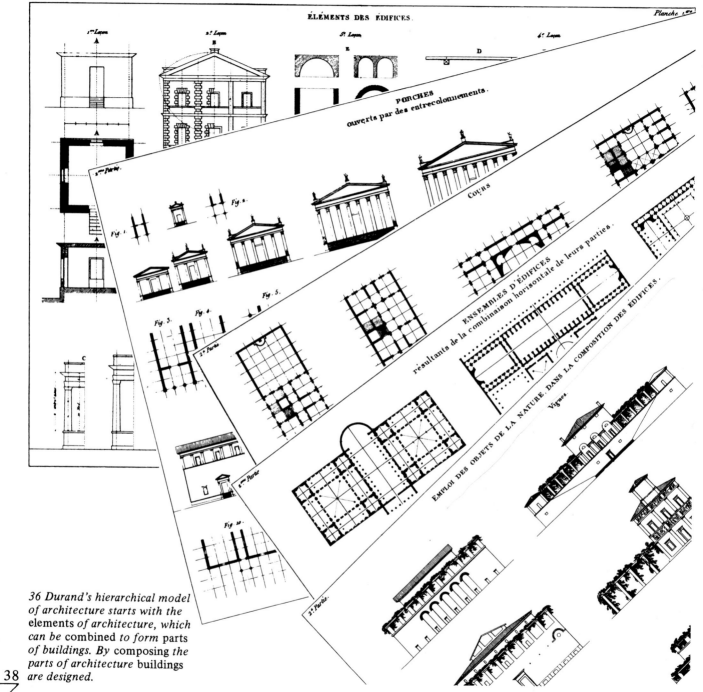

36 Durand's hierarchical model
of architecture starts with the
elements of architecture, which
can be combined to form parts
of buildings. By composing the
parts of architecture buildings
are designed.

38

"If you treat each new project as a completely new study, then after working on a few projects, laziness or vanity will inevitably reduce you to a few particular patterns of ideas which will afterwards be repeated in all projects you do, even those for which they are quite unsuitable. If instead of working only on projects, you first study the principles of architecture and become familiar with the mechanism of composition, you will be able with ease and success to do a project of any type whatever."
Durand, *Precis* (vol. 2), 1817[32]

What then is composition? "Composition is, in plain English, 'putting together'..."[33] states Ruskin, afraid perhaps of the academic implications of the verb 'to compose'. A more sympathetic exponent of composition in architecture and the last Grand Professeur of the Beaux Arts tradition, Julien Guadet, defined it a century after the publication of Durand's *Precis*: "Composer, c'est faire l'emploit de ce qu'on sait"[34]— to compose is to make use of what is known.

"How to compose, if you are not familiar with the objects that have to be composed? How to imagine any building if you have no idea of the parts out of which it must be formed and if you do not also know how those parts should be combined?"[35]— asked Durand. Those questions were not rhetorical. The answers were provided by the generation of alternative architectural forms out of a fixed, exact vocabulary, and the systematic exploration of different assemblies of those forms, presented during his profusely illustrated lectures. Durand in his early lessons explained design as a process of composing with a predetermined parts; "Before Composition one should know with which elements we compose, since the composition of the totality of the building is nothing but the result of assemblage of its parts, which in turn are made by the elements of the building, the walls, the roofs, etc."[36]

Among the important design procedures governing his assemblage of parts were, regulating lines, harmonic and modular proportions, axes of symmetry and grids. While the elements were well defined, the "partis" and their assemblies remained on a schematic level. These implicit rules enriched by other procedures like mirroring, rotational symmetries, harmonic repetitions etc., soon became part of Beaux Arts system. The vocabulary used with these procedures was rooted in the classical orders and remained neo-classical or crypto-neo-classical until the dessemination of non-objective art in our century.

Durand's interpretation of the City was a natural extension of his systematic, generative structure of architecture. "De meme que les murs, les colonnes, etc., sont les elements dont se composent les edifices, de meme les edifices sont les elements dont se composent les villes,"[38] — just as walls, columns, etc. are the elements from which buildings are composed, so buildings are the elements from which towns are composed.

"There is one great difference between the French system and our own, and it not only applies to architecture but to every other art, and that is, the entire absence in England of any study of composition, and of the complete way it is taught in France... The English student makes no sketch-design; he begins at once with his two-foot rule to put the exact size of every feature in the building, without going a step further in the study of design."
An advocate of an classicist English academy, writing in 1884[37]

37 Plan generation through systematic combination of square, rectangle and circle, Durand, 1802

41

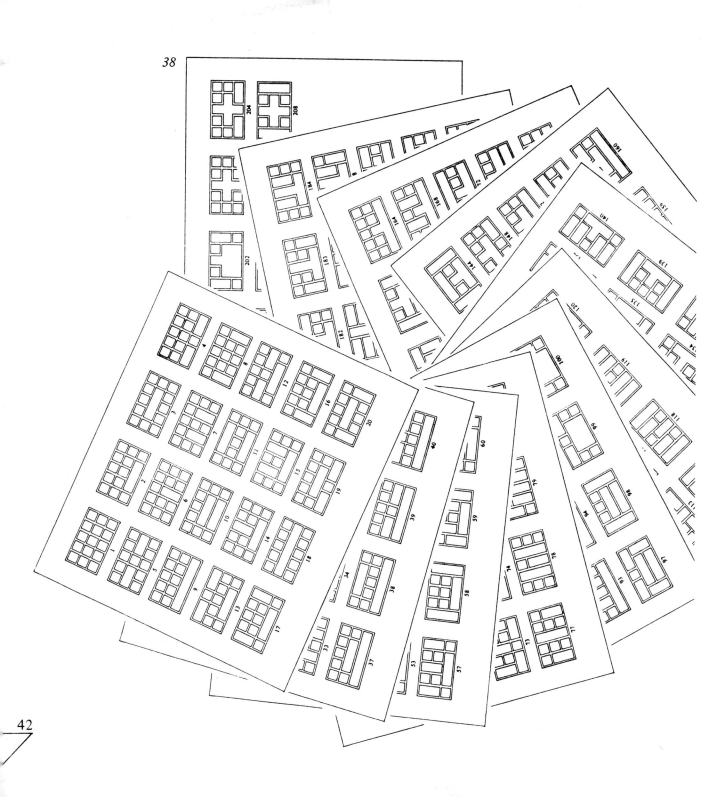

38 A shape grammar generated catalogue of Palladian plans, by Stiny & Mitchell. The Villa Malcontenta corresponds to no. 204.

"Even the small fragments of generative grammars that now exist are incomparably greater in explicit coverage than traditional or structuralist descriptions... A generative grammar is simply one that gives explicit rules that determine the structure of sentences... The limitations of generative grammars are limitations of our knowledge... Where traditional or structuralist descriptions are correct, they can immediately be incorporated into generative grammars."

Noam Chomsky, 1965[40]

2. Shape Grammars [39]

The analogy between language and architecture is long-established. The study of language has seen dramatic developments in recent years, and it is natural to consider applying new ideas from linguistics to the study of architecture. One aspect, semiotics, deals with meaning. Another, generative grammars, is concerned with the mechanism of constructing sentences: shape grammars follow this model. The fundamental idea of generative grammars is that every speaker of a language uses **precise** rules to generate new sentences; if he relied solely on experience he could only repeat what he heard before. The task of linguistics is to decompose language and specify exactly what its generating rules are.

Shape Grammars are a close analogy, applied to the generation of shapes rather than sentences. A Shape Grammar is a set of precise generating rules. The rules can be used in varied ways, to produce a language of shapes. Each Shape Grammar has its own language of shapes: Shape Grammars are not linked to any particular formal vocabulary or style.

Linguistics is primarily concerned with analysis, not with the invention of new languages. Similarly, the first applications of Shape Grammars have been in analysis or criticism. Typically, a given building or style is taken, and shape rules induced that can re-generate the given shapes. The same rules can then, of course, generate new shapes in the language of the original. It is an effective, operational way of making precedents available for creative re-use: this is what we have done in "Topics in Architecture".

43

Shape Grammar

A shape grammar is a set of generating rules to create shapes. Generation begins with an initial shape, which is transformed by applying the shape rules until a finished shape is reached. One shape grammar can create many shapes – sometimes infinitely many; the grammar together with the shapes it can generate can be called a design language.

A shape rule consists of a left-hand side and a right-hand side. The rule can be applied to a given shape if it contains a sub-shape which matches the LHS of the rule; when the rule is applied the sub-shape is replaced by another sub-shape corresponding to the RHS of the rule. For example, if we have a shape rule like this

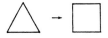

it can be applied to a given shape thus.

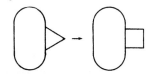

Normally changes of scale, rotation, and mirroring are permitted when matching the LHS of a rule to a sub-shape; but the scale, orientation of the sub-shape must be preserved when applying the rule.

Shape grammars that create drawings deal with 2-dimensional shapes, but 3-dimensional shape grammars are possible, as are 1-dimensional ones. They can be applied by hand, but since the recognition of LHS matching, and the application of LHS to RHS transformations are quite mechanical tasks, computer aids suggest themselves. Computer-based 2- and 3-dimensional shape grammars are complex, but a 1-dimensional shape grammar can be simulated by a conventional word-processor.

Word-processors have a "replace" function, which scans a file of text for a specified sequence of characters and replaces it with another sequence. For example in the following file
CbSbSbRbSbT
we could instruct **bRb** to be replaced by **bLb**, giving
CbSbSbLbSbT

If we ask the processor to replace **bSb** with **bSbSb**, it starts at the left and identifies the first instance of **bSb**, and asks whether to make the replacement or ignore it; then it would go on to the second instance, and ask again, and finally go to the third. If we told it to ignore the first two, but to replace the third we get
CbSbSbLbSbSbT

Replace instructions in a word-processor have a LHS and a RHS directly analogous to shape rules. They operate on characters in a computer file, but these characters can of course be a symbolic representation of shapes. For example, **b** might be a bridge-like shape, and **bSb** might be two bridges connecting to a tower in a straight line.

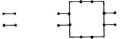

A replace rule **b → bSb** corresponds to a shape rule

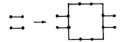

With a set of replace rules we can generate and operate on a string of symbols; in effect, this is an operational shape grammar for a class of 1-dimensional shapes:

I	C	→ Cb
II	b	→ bSb
III	b	→ bLb
IV	b	→ bRb
V	b	→ bT
VI	bSb	→ bLb
VII	bSb	→ bRb
VIII	bRb	→ bSb
IX	bLb	→ bSb

Here are a number of stages in the generation of a shape, starting with **C** :

	I	II	II	IV	III	V	IX
C	⇒Cb	⇒CbSb	⇒CbSbSb	⇒CbSbSbRb	⇒CbSbSbRbLb	⇒CbSbSbRbLbT	⇒CbSbSbRbSbT

Some rules add elements to the string, whilst others make changes. Rules which take objects away are also possible, like **bSbSb → b**. But the methods of representing rules and applying them are just the same.

Using the word-processor/shape grammar an infinite number of symbol strings and plans can be generated with nine rules.

An example of generation is shown below, in which the final string is one of the possible linear compositions of Kahn's Richards Laboratories plan components.

Here we assume the letters are just symbols for the shapes, but of course they could be statements in a computer language (like LOGO) that can draw the shapes they represent. The word-processor generates a program to draw the shape. This is in principle what happens in CAD graphic systems, which store a drawing as the set of commands that generate it, not literally as the set of screen coordinates in the visual image.

But this is only the beginning of the potential of Shape Grammars. By making alterations to a given Shape Grammar the language of shapes is modified, maybe subtly or maybe radically.[41] In this way it is possible to model the incremental development of style, typical of the history of ideas and art.

The great advances offered by Shape Grammars lie in two main directions: first, its precision — it is a more precise methodology for the generation of form than earlier approaches and can handle in an exact way formal ideas that are otherwise vague; and secondly, its generality — it is stylistically neutral, treating all styles equally and concentrating on internal consistency. It is **both** rigorous and eclectic.

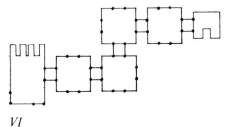

VI
⇨ **CbSbLbRbSbT**

Durand + Shape Grammar → Design Expert System

Expert systems are applied artificial intelligence, ie. they resemble aspects of human expertise and intelligence. One important aspect is flexibility – the way that humans bring a variety of different kinds of knowledge to bear on a problem. Durand's hierarchy and Shape Grammars are in one sense alternative approaches: can they be combined in an expert system?

An ideal expert system for architectural design should know about all the aspects of formal structure that we have encountered. It should be able to store objects, both primitive and composite, as in Durand; it should be able to store rules, as in Shape Grammars; and it should be able to use them in different strategies – composition or decomposition, top-down or bottom-up.

Expert systems are made up of many individual pieces of knowledge, typically held as IF ... THEN ... relations, called production rules. Can the varied requirements of an architectural expert system fit within this uniform format?

A shape rule of course fits very simply into the format. But suppose the IF ... part of a shape rule is empty: this implies the THEN ... part is **always** true, ie. is a fact. In this way it is possible to describe objects, as in Durand.

If objects and rules can both be represented, what about different design strategies? First, composition is the process of developing or elaborating a current design: this involves applying shape rules so that the IF ... part of a clause matches the current design, and replacing it with the THEN ... part. Often there may be many matching shape rules, and the designer has to decide which to apply. And decomposition is just the opposite: matching the THEN ... part of a shape rule against the current design and replacing it with the IF ... part. Again, there may be alternative ways of decomposing a design.

Top-down and bottom-up strategies derive from the content of the generating rules used. Top-down rules are typically **transformational,** whereas bottom-up rules are **additive.** Both types of rule can be used for composition and equally for decomposition.

So the significant issues we have identified can in principle be handled by a knowledge-based expert system using production rules.

Furthermore IF ... THEN ... clauses are quite versatile. Not all conditions or consequents have to be shapes, but can relate to other attributes of interest, eg. dimensions or functional restrictions, etc. The THEN ... part could even be a warning or a piece of advice. So interactive consultation and criticism can be handled within production rules.

If the internal organisation of an architectural expert system can be relatively uniform, what are its main functional components? The following layers correspond to the architectural knowledge that would have to be held in the system, and to a user's access to it.

Database The system must have a large data-base of architectural objects, rules or strategies, either on-line or stored in a library.

Context But in a given design only part (usually a small part) of the database will be relevant: the user selects items from the database for the current context. New items created in a context can themselves be added to the database.

Current design Within the context there can be one or more designs, but the system operates on one design at a time. The current design can be developed or analysed by applying rules from the context, or by direct user manipulation.

The options open to the user of such a system can be imagined as a tree structure. When working on a design it would be highly interactive: the mode of operation is to identify by pattern-matching opportunities to which the user reacts; the system implements the kind of computer graphics workstation that is already available.

The design expert system that we have sketched does not yet exist, but we predict that it will. Until it does, we cannot know what designs it will assist in creating ...

"Unhappily architecture is not the art of doing a certain number of projects; it is the art of doing all possible projects."
Durand *Partie graphique*, 1821[42]
"A generative grammar is not concerned with any *actual* set of sentences in the language but with the *possible* set of sentences."
Frank Palmer *Grammar*, 1971[43]

In conclusion both methodologies, Shape Grammar as well as Durand's, are found to be probabilistic systems: they establish constraints on the generation of form within which choice and variety can exist. Generating rules are more explicit and precise in the case of Shape Grammars than with Durand. Yet in the latter's system of architectural notation lies much of its usefulness, despite its limits. Durand's "partis" are few and can therefore be illustrated in form of a catalogue or database of formal precedents, intuitively comprehensible and applicable in design. For the language of a Shape Grammar, the catalogue is impossible to examine due to its size, and thus constrained generation and reductive modelling are needed. Both methodologies can be applied to composing and decomposing architectural objects, as generating or analytical tools. **That is, both can be engaged in the reading and writing of architecture.**

The forms composed and decomposed with Durand's method, as well as those using Shape Grammars, confirm the importance of **structured assembly** in design procedures. Jacob Bronowski in his penetrating discussion of human ascent, proposed: "I am making a basic separation between architecture as moulding and architecture as assembly of parts. That seems a very simple distinction: the mud house, the stone masonry. But **in fact it represents a fundamental intellectual difference**, not just technical one."[44]

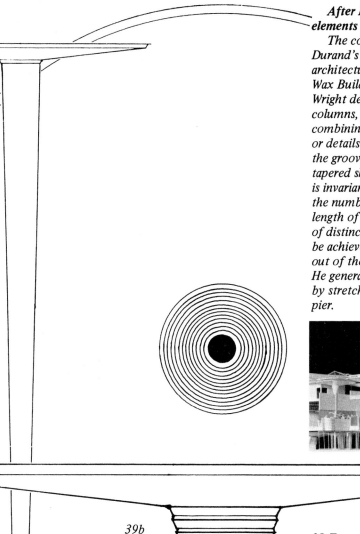

39a

39b

After Durand: details and elements

The column is one of Durand's basic elements of architecture. In the Johnson Wax Building, Frank Lloyd Wright designed a family of columns, made up by combining three sub-elements or details – the circular head, the grooved capital, and the tapered shaft. The circular head is invariant, but by interchanging the number of grooves and the length of the shaft a number of distinct column-heights can be achieved. Wright used four out of the thirteen possibiliites. He generated further columns by stretching the shaft into a pier.

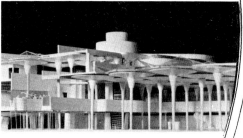

39 Two columns not found in the Johnson Wax Building, a: the tallest possible, b: the shortest.
40 Columns used by Wright in Johnson Wax.

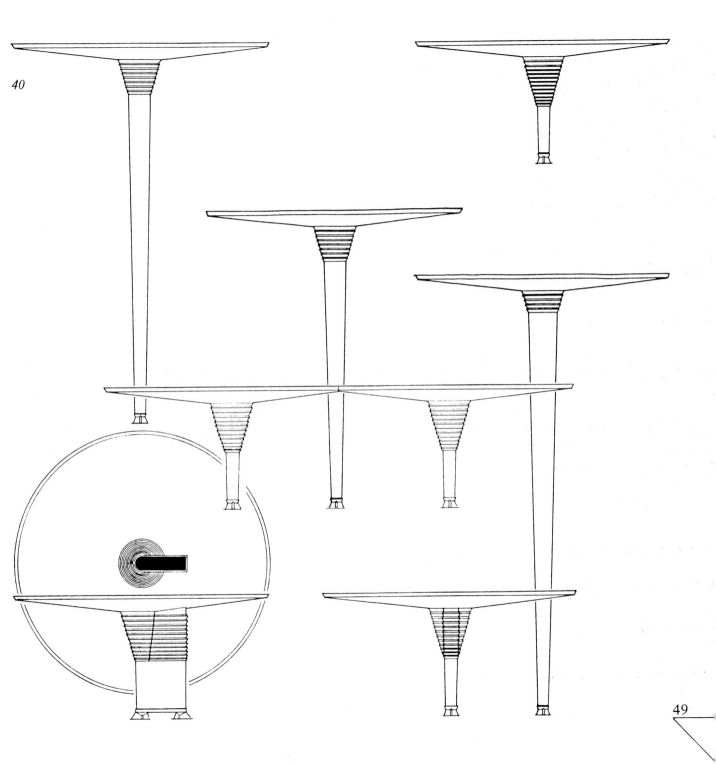

40

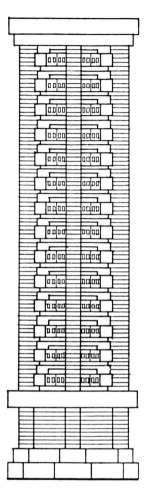

After Durand: combination of elements

The combination of building elements is one stage in Durand's hierarchy of design. At the Imperial Hotel in Tokyo, Frank Lloyd Wright designed a cruciform column which is combined with parapet walls and other architectural elements. Combinations are governed by a square planning grid, and permissible combinations can be enumerated. The whole building is symmetrical and was drawn on squared paper – the identical discipline to that used by Durand's pupils. But unlike Durand's pupils Wright used an original, non-classical vocabulary.

45

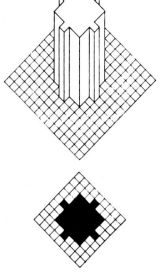

41

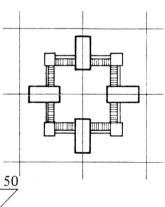

50

41 Wright's cruciform column from the Imperial Hotel; elevation and plan.
42 Eleven ways of combining the column and a parapet wall.
43 Examples of the column being combined with other architectural elements, from the Imperial Hotel.
44 Combination of columns and parapet walls in a gallery over the entrance lobby, Imperial Hotel.
45 Combination of columns and walls, from Durand.

42

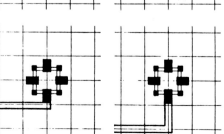

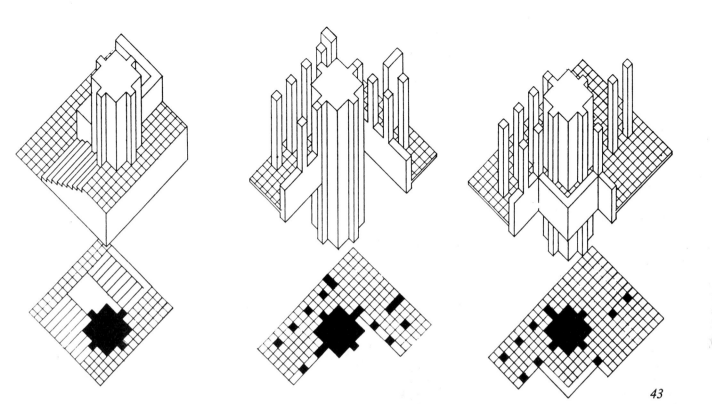

43

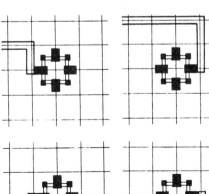

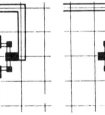

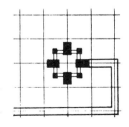

44

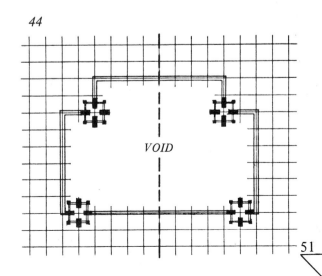

VOID

51

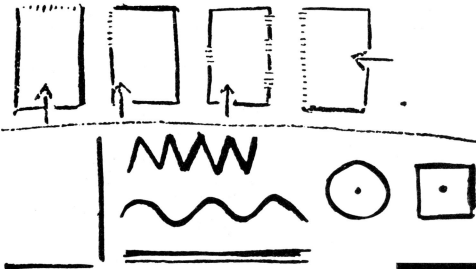

***After Durand: elements and
parts***

Le Corbusier's sketch shows
a spatial type which can lead to
considerable variety. The type is
similar to the courtrooms at his
High Court of Justice,
Chandigarh. In Durand's terms,
the room can be considered a
part of a building, made up of
the **elements** door, wall, and sun
screen. For elements of given
dimensions, and for given ways
of combining them, the
possible building parts can be
enumerated.

46 Sketch by Le Corbusier.

ELEMENTS

door	wall	screen

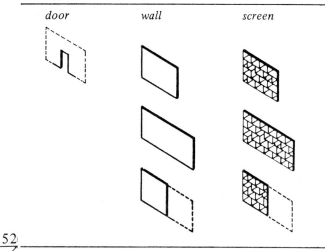

COMBINATIONS OF ELEMENTS

door and wall	wall and screen

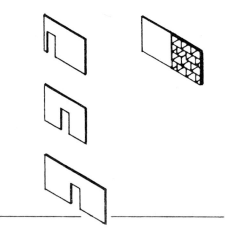

One screen element   Two screen elements

door in end of short wall

door in centre of short wall

door in centre of long wall

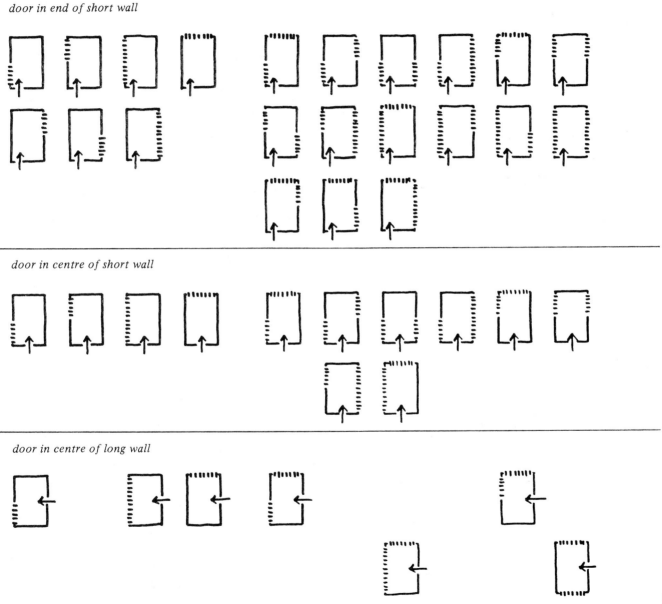

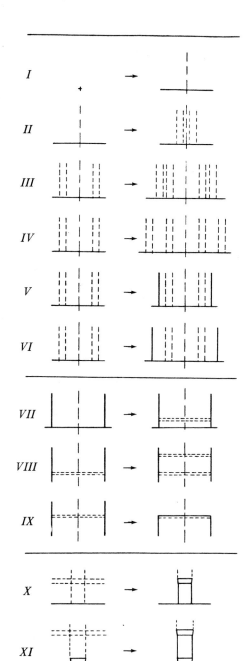

Shape Grammar: building components

Shape Grammars can be used to represent the rules governing the setting-out of building components – for example the masonry in the outer elevations of Louis Kahn's Exeter College Library, where all dimensions are regulated by the precise size of the bricks. Starting from a null initial shape, vertical and horizontal grids are generated, determining the number of bays and stories. Then the masonry is set out, with shape rules to determine the pattern of vertical and horizontal courses. Using the Shape Grammar an infinite number of elevations can be designed with exactly the same way of using masonry components.

47 Kahn's masonry elevation of Exeter College Library.
48,49 New elevations designed with shape rules derived from Kahn's elevation.

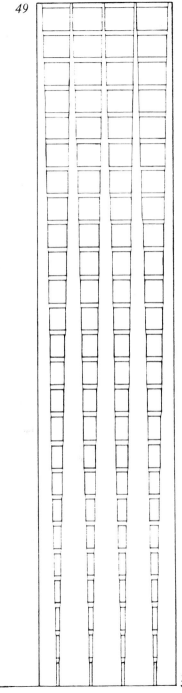

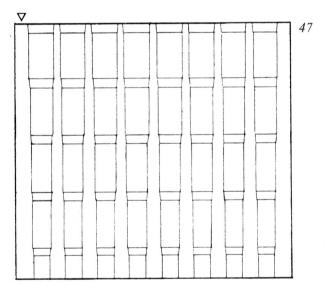

47

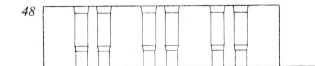

48

49

55

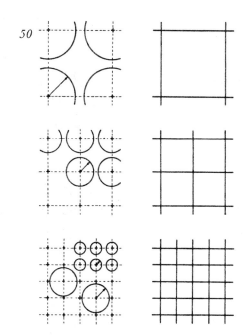

50

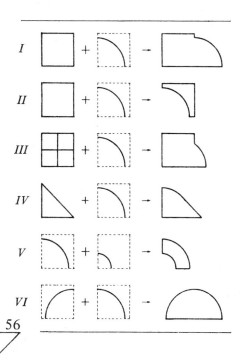

I   □ + ◜ → ◗

II   □ + ◜ → ◝

III   ⊞ + ◜ → ◗

IV   ◺ + ◜ → ◿

V   ◜ + ◝ → ◞

VI   ◠ + ◜ → ◠

Shape Grammar: regulating geometry

A Shape Grammar can be used to represent the abstract regulating geometry of a design – the geometry which determines the disposition of building elements, but which is lost in the finished design. Wright's Johnson Wax Building has two regulating geometries, square and circular, and their combination gives the design is geometrical sophistication. A Shape Grammar gives rules for combining elements from the geometries, and can be illustrated by a fragment of Wright's design. The variety of designs that could be generated by a Johnson Wax Shape Grammar is infinite.

50 The regulating grids used by Wright in the Johnson Wax Building.
51 Fragment of Wright's design, showing the combination of geometries.

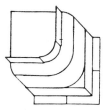

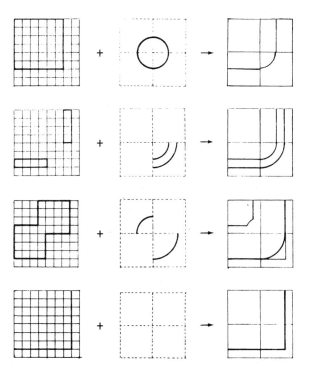

51

"Every house worth considering as a work of art must have a grammar of its own... You must be consistently grammatical for it to be understood as a work of Art. Consistency of grammar is therefore the property — solely — of the well-developed artist-architect... A man who designs the house must, inevitably, speak a consistent thought-language in his design. It may be and properly should be a language of his own if appropriate. If he has no language, so no grammar, of his own, he must adopt one."
Frank Lloyd Wright, *The Natural House*, 1954[45]

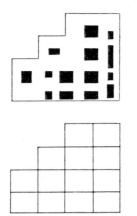

53

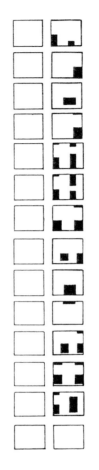

54

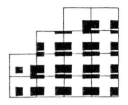
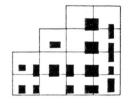

55

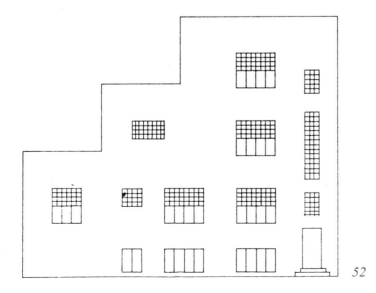

52

52 Elevation of the Scheu House, Vienna, by Adolf Loos, 1912-13.
53 Decomposition of Loos's design.
54 "Tiles" derived from Loos's design.
55 New compositions of the "tiles".

57

56 Analytical drawing of a
Le Corbusier painting by
Bernard Hoesli, explaining the
compositional method employed.

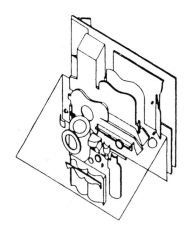

"The whole methodology is based upon the development of 'combinations' and 'assemblages' of lines, planes and volumes, independent of what the given elements may represent. Just as an appropriate assembly of sounds gives us musical products, so too we assemble a representation in which lines, planes & volumes can be musically tuned. Thus we create a skilled composer of new forms".
Iakov Chernikhov, *The Construction of Architectural and Machine Forms,* 1931[46]

Even the most disciplined of architectural styles, French academic classicism, barely made its rules, or its grammar, explicit. "Any complete building whatever is not, and cannot be, anything but the result of the assembly and putting together (composition) of a greater or lesser number of parts," said Gaudet, Professor at the Beaux-Arts. But Banham notes, "The specific mode of putting the parts together is something that Gaudet barely discusses... The fact was, simply that the symmetrical disposition of the parts of the building about one or more axes was so unquestionably the master-discipline of academic architecture that there was no need for him to discuss it."
Reyner Banham, *Theory and design in the first machine age,* 1960[47]

Finale

"To compose is to make use of what is known," said Guadet. Of course he knew only the neo-classical vocabulary of the Beaux-Arts architecture and he thought and made to be sure, is more engaging than composition, nothing more seductive. It is the true realm of the artist with no limits... What is it to compose? It is to put together, weld, unite, the parts of the whole. These parts, in their turn, are elements of architecture".[48] Based on such sentiments the frozen classical method and its equally stable vocabulary resulted in the collapse of the Beaux-Arts tradition.

The limiting aspects of the Academy were clear to the early Modernists. In the writings of the influential Soviet avant-garde architect Iakov Chernikov, for example, the notion of composition is carefully avoided and substituted with a new motto: "**Constructivism** as a concept relates to any combination of different objects capable of being brought together into a single unified entity."[49] He proceeds to recognise four types of constructive procedure, amalgamation, combination, assemblage, and conjugation. All these operations would have made Durand quite comfortable. In terms of **method**, continuity with the Academy is self-evident, but unacknowledged. The early modernists could be called crypto-classicists with a non-objective vocabulary.

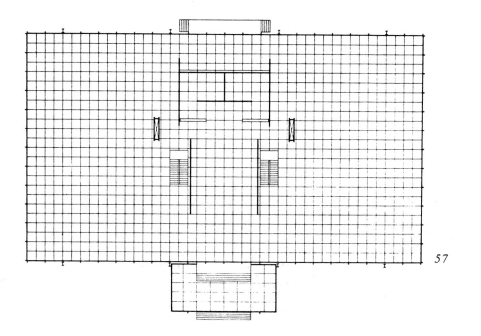

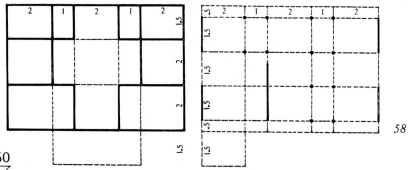

57

57 Classical grid and symmetry in
the work of Mies van der Rohe.
(Crown Hall, IIT)
58 Similarity of proportional grids
in Villa Malcontenta, Palladio, C16
(left), and Villa Stein,
Le Corbusier, 1927 (right).

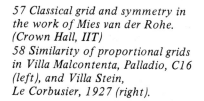

58

"... consider whether, after all, architectural theory does not stand very much where it stood in 1920, or 1800, or even 1750, and whether the position of an architect who is concerned about expression or style is not that of a man feeling his way back to classicism or neo-classicism, or, to put the finest possible point on it, crypto-neo-classicism." John Summerson, *The Case for a theory of modern architecture,* 1957[50]

Their formal vocabulary was revolutionary, yet amazingly coherent, consisting of a self-referential set of formal elements and parts, white and abstract (see Weissenhof[51]). The disposition of those elements was subjected to classical manipulations like regulating lines, grids, axes, shifted grids, rotations. Bilateral symmetry, with the exception of Mies' late work, was illegal and elements were composed in a "free" manner. Furthermore, the modern parts and elements were not drawn from architectural precedents, but were based on great individual formal discoveries, the machine aesthetic and painterly search. An explicit design method was no longer legitimate and many design innovations could not be passed on. Twenty years elapsed from the completion of the Villa Stein at Garches (1927) to Colin Rowe's explanation of its deeper structure (1947). It took another twenty-five years for "The Mathematics of the Ideal Villa"[52] to be used as text by students of architecture. The disposition of Modern elements was never self-concious or recorded in rule forms. It was a private domain; the artist of the Jazz decades was engaged in invention and improvisation, ignoring even modest advances of other designers. If the first generation of modernists carried over their pre-modern training, they did not pass it on. Succeeding generations of architects worked in complete ignorance of classical compositional methods, until the recent reintroduction of precedent, memory and typology to design.

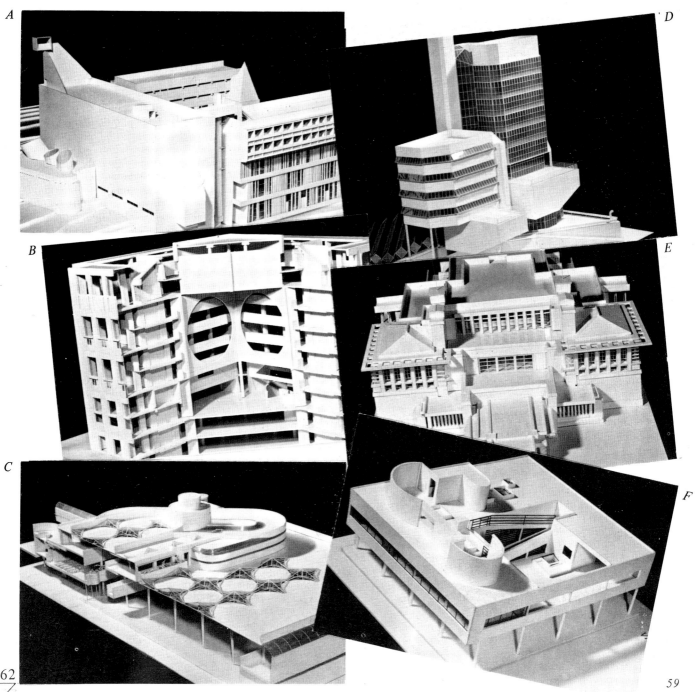

59 Student models from
"Topics in Architecture".
(key overleaf)

A notable exception can be found in the essay "Investigations in collective form" written twenty years ago by Fumihiko Maki. After establishing three principles of collective form, Compositional Form, Mega-Structure Form, and Group-Form, Maki made a penetrating observation on the compositional approach: "The elements which comprise a compositional form are preconceived and predetermined separately."[53]

Mies (who via Schinkel is distant relative of Durand) spoke of method in his IIT address: "Education must lead us from irresponsible opinion to the responsible judgment. It must lead us from change and arbitrariness, to rational clarity of intellectual orders".[54] In spite of talk of intellectual orders, he never made his own explicit. A fact which of course did not prevent his compositions being widely copied.

As Aldo Rossi observed recently: "If we refer to the modern movement, the most important architects are those who created the possibility of repetition. For instance, Mies van der Rohe. For me Mies van der Rohe is one of the greatest architects simply because many of the buildings, some beautiful and some ugly, which have conquered the enterprise of modern cities, are copies descending from Mies van der Rohe. But Mies did not teach method; he made some buildings which become models, and which have been models for one generation."[55]

60 Collage of "Hong Kong" skyline, with student models from "Topics in Architecture", 1980-81.

Key to Figure 59
A Le Corbusier, La Tourette
B Louis Kahn, Exeter Library
C Frank Lloyd Wright, Johnson Wax Administration Building
D Stirling & Gowan, Leicester University Engineering Building
E Frank Lloyd Wright, Imperia Hotel, Tokyo
F Le Corbusier, Villa Savoye
G Le Corbusier, High Court of Justice, Chandigarh
H Louis Kahn, Richards Medica Research Laboratories
I Mies van der Rohe, Crown Hall, IIT

Another comment on the importance of precedent and the limits of the structured approach to design comes from Libeskind's essay on the "Deconstruction of Architecture": "The interpretation of past architecture is dependent on a structural "reading", but only as means towards the poetic end of Architecture. The semantic level and its historical reality constitutes the richness of content and demands a further level of questioning, **of making.**"[56]

Today while the see-saw of architectural demi-monde swings between canonically exclusive "Hooked on Classics" and randomly inclusive "Punk Rock", or at best between composition and decomposition, the notion of explicit design procedures regains its importance.

The application of what have, until now, been mutually exclusive design approaches is of central importance: top-down vs. bottom-up, welding vs. splitting, uniting vs. separating, writing vs. reading, or composition vs. decomposition.

Because,
IF: "To compose is to make use of what is known",[57]
THEN: To decompose is to make known what is.
And,
IF: "A novel is a machine for generating interpretations",[58]
THEN: Architecture is ...

65

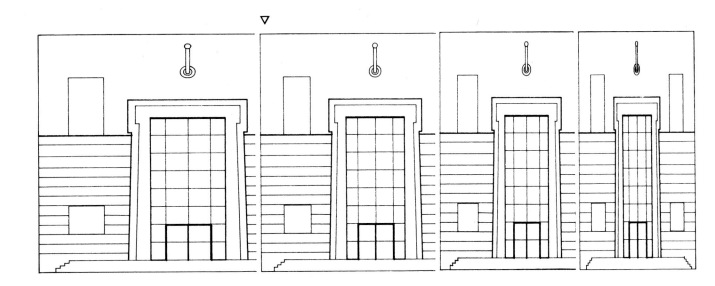

*61 Computer generated variations
of the Entry to Stockholm Public
Library, G Asplund, 1924
(original design marked ▽).*

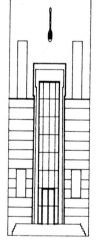

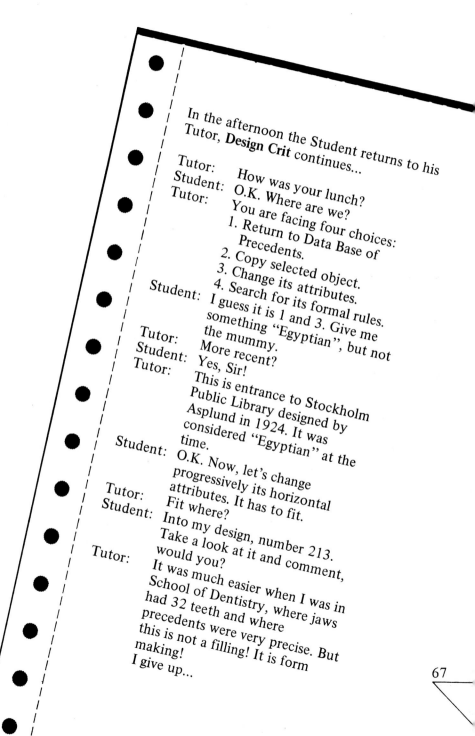

In the afternoon the Student returns to his Tutor, **Design Crit** continues...

Tutor: How was your lunch?

Student: O.K. Where are we?

Tutor: You are facing four choices:
1. Return to Data Base of Precedents.
2. Copy selected object.
3. Change its attributes.
4. Search for its formal rules.

Student: I guess it is 1 and 3. Give me something "Egyptian", but not the mummy.

Tutor: More recent?

Student: Yes, Sir!

Tutor: This is entrance to Stockholm Public Library designed by Asplund in 1924. It was considered "Egyptian" at the time.

Student: O.K. Now, let's change progressively its horizontal attributes. It has to fit.

Tutor: Fit where?

Student: Into my design, number 213. Take a look at it and comment, would you?

Tutor: It was much easier when I was in School of Dentistry, where jaws had 32 teeth and where precedents were very precise. But this is not a filling! It is form making!
I give up...

62 Computer generated
LOOSASPLUDSOOL Pastiche.

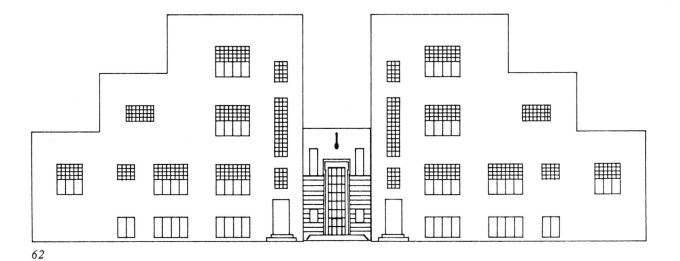

62

And with the final word "pastiche!" flashing across the screen the system aborts. Student desparate to produce a solution in time for jury reaches for system manual and examines Tutor's structure.

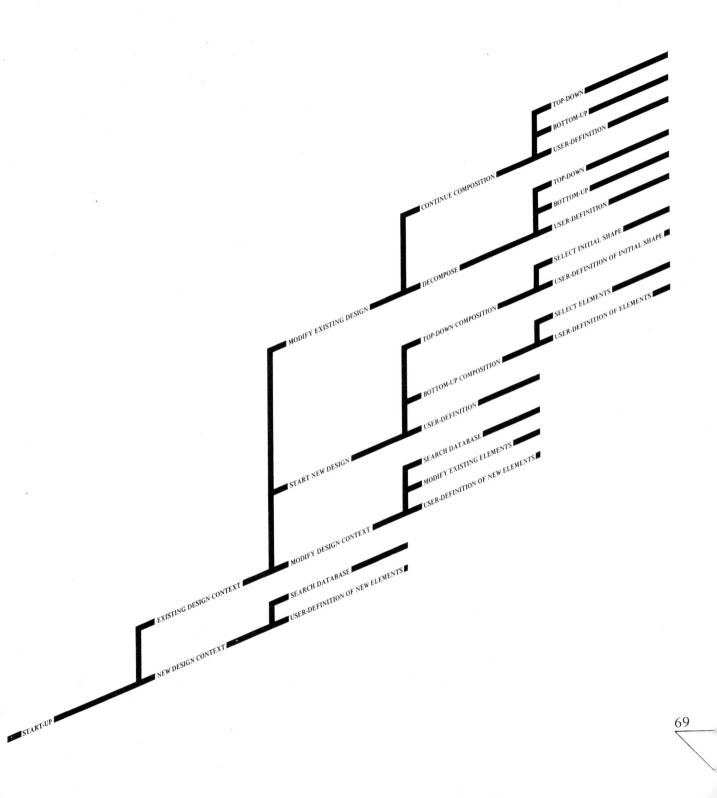

START-UP

NEW DESIGN CONTEXT

EXISTING DESIGN CONTEXT

USER-DEFINITION OF NEW ELEMENTS

SEARCH DATABASE

MODIFY DESIGN CONTEXT

START NEW DESIGN

MODIFY EXISTING DESIGN

USER-DEFINITION OF NEW ELEMENTS

MODIFY EXISTING ELEMENTS

SEARCH DATABASE

USER-DEFINITION

BOTTOM-UP COMPOSITION

TOP-DOWN COMPOSITION

DECOMPOSE

CONTINUE COMPOSITION

SELECT ELEMENTS

USER-DEFINITION OF ELEMENTS

SELECT INITIAL SHAPE

USER-DEFINITION OF INITIAL SHAPE

TOP-DOWN

BOTTOM-UP

USER-DEFINITION

TOP-DOWN

BOTTOM-UP

USER-DEFINITION

Finally student loads Expert Design System
and invokes the on-screen response;

Design Crit II...

Tutor: Hi! What are you working on?
Student: I have the new idea.
Tutor: Let's see it... It's a small one.
Student: Shall I zoom in?
Tutor: Apart from zoom, other possible
design procedures are: translate,
rotate, mirror, layer, change
attributes, decompose, compose
and last but not least ... erase.

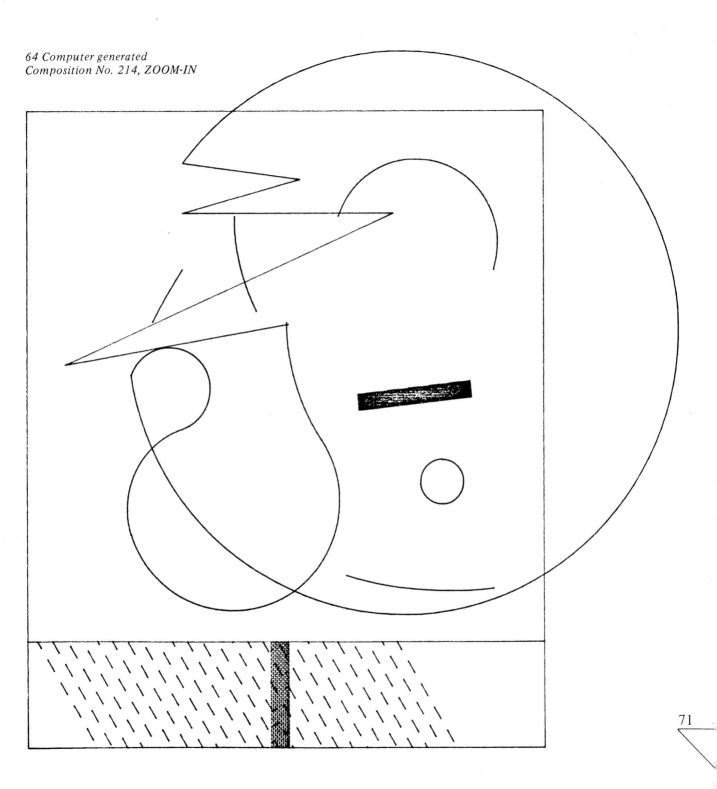

64 Computer generated
Composition No. 214, ZOOM-IN

71

Acknowledgements and References

The material in this essay was first presented in the "Topics in Architecture" course, to Year Four students studying for the Bachelor of Architecture degree in Hong Kong University Department of Architecture. The authors would like to thank Professor K C Lye, who established the course; and the students who participated in the "Topics in Architecture" Seminars, where much of the illustrative material was generated.

At the Seminars the students described and analysed the following ten buildings:

Frank Lloyd Wright, Imperial Hotel, Tokyo, 1915-22

Le Corbusier, Villa Savoye, Poissy, 1929-31

Frank Lloyd Wright, Johnson Wax Administration Building, Racine, Wis, 1936-39; 1947-50

Alvar Aalto, Saynatsalo Town Hall, 1949-52

Mies van der Rohe, Crown Hall, Illinois Institute of Technology, Chicago, Ill, 1950-56

Le Corbusier, High Court of Justice, Chandigarh, 1951-56

Le Corbusier, Monastery of La Tourette, Eveux 1956-60

Louis Kahn, Richards Medical Research Laboratories, University of Pennsylvania, 1957-60

James Stirling & James Gowan, Engineering Building, Leicester University, 1959-64

Louis Kahn, Exeter College Library, Exeter, N.H., 1968-72

References

1 D Knuth "Computer science and mathematics" *American Scientist* vol. 61, 1975 (p. 709)

2 *The Concise Oxford Dictionary of Music* Oxford: University Press, 1980 (p. 142)

3 Ibid (p. 201)

4 C. Shannon & W. Weaver *The Mathematical Theory of Communication* Urbana, Ill.: Illinois University Press, 1949 (pp. 43-44)

5 Arnold Schoenberg *Fundamentals of Musical Composition* London: Faber, 1976 (p. 1)

6 Ibid (p. 215)

7 J. Silvetti *Lotus* no. 18, 1977

8 Viollet le Duc *Dictionnaire Raisonne de l'Architecture Francaise* Paris, 1866

9 Louis Kahn, communicated by Manuel Vicente

10 W.S.H. Hung *A Complete Course in the Art of Chinese Calligraphy* Hong Kong: Michael Stevenson, 1984 (p. 203)

11 Sir Joshua Reynolds *Discourses on Art* ed. R.R. Walk, New Haven, N.J.: Yale University Press, 1975 (Discourse VI, On Imitation, 1774)

12 Ibid

13 Ibid

14 Ibid

15 Jean-Nicholas-Louis Durand *Partie graphique des cours d'architecture faits a l'Ecole Royale Polytechnique* Paris, 1821 (Photo-reprint with *Precis des lecons d'architecture donnes a l'Ecole Royale Polytechnique* 2nd. edn., Paris, 1817-19, by Verlag Dr Alfons Uhl, Noerdlingen, 1981)

16 C. Hussey *Life of Sir Edwin Lutyens* London: Country Life, 1950 (p. 133)

17 N. Negroponte *Soft Architecture Machines* Cambridge, Mass: MIT Press, 1975 (p. 145)

18 "Typology" *Encyclopaedia Britannica*

19 John Ruskin *The Stones of Venice* London, 1851

20 The notion of replacement of type with prototype is first discussed by Rafael Moneo in his article "On Typology" *Oppositions* no. 13, 1978 (pp. 23-45)

21 Quatremere de Quincy *Dictionnaire Historique de l'Architecture* Paris, 1832

22 Moneo, op cit

23 A. Rossi *A Scientific Autobiography* Cambridge, Mass: MIT Press, 1981 (p. 23)

24 N. Chomsky, from a paper read in 1965, reprinted in J.P.B. Allen & P. Van Buren *Chomsky: Selected Readings* London: Oxford University Press, 1971 (p. 153)

25 Durand *Precis* op cit

26 "Topics in Architecture" is a lecture/seminar course in the theory of design offered by the authors at Hong Kong University Department of Architecture.

27 A. Branham *The Architecture of the French Enlightenment* London: Thames and Hudson, 1980 (p. 225)

28 L. Benevolo *History of Modern Architecture* Cambridge, Mass: MIT Press, 1977 (vol. 1, p. 34)

29 K. Frampton *Modern Architecture: a Critical History* London: Thames and Hudson, 1980 (p. 15)

30 D. Watkin *The Rise of Architectural History* London: Architectural Press, 1980 (p. 23)

31 Durand *Precis* op cit

32 Ibid

33 Ruskin, op cit

34 Julien Gaudet *Elements et Theories de l'Architecture* Paris, 1902

35 Durand *Precis* op cit

36 Ibid

37 Quoted in R. Macleod *Style and Society* London: RIBA Publications, 1971 (p. 91)

38 Durand *Precis* op cit

39 G. Stiny "An Introduction to shape and shape grammars" *Environment & Planning B* vol. 7, 1980 (pp. 343-352)

40 N. Chomsky, op cit (p. 157)

41　T.W. Knight "Languages of designs: from known to new" *Environment & Planning B* vol. 8, 1981 (pp. 213-238)

42　Durand *Partie graphique* op cit

43　F. Palmer *Grammar* London: Penguin, 1971 (p. 150)

44　J. Bronowski *The Ascent of Man* London: Macdonald Futura, 1973 (p. 57)

45　Frank Lloyd Wright *The Natural House* 1954; reprinted in *Writings and Buildings* Cleveland, Ohio: Meridian Books 1960 (pp. 296-297)

46　I. Chernikov *The Construction of Architectural and Machine Forms* 1931; published in *Architectural Design* no. 11/12, 1984

47　R Banham *Theory and Design in the First Machine Age* London: Architectural Press, 1960 (p. 16)

48　Guadet, op cit

49　Chernikov, op cit

50　J. Summerson "The Case for a theory of modern architecture" *RIBA Journal* vol. 64, June 1957 (pp. 307-313)

51　Weissenhof was a building exhibition in Stuttgart in 1927, directed by Mies van der Rohe, where many first generation Modern architects participated; see Frampton, op cit (p. 163)

52　C. Rowe *The Mathematics of the Ideal Villa and Other Essays* Cambridge, Mass: MIT Press, 1976

53　F. Maki *Investigations in Collective Form* St Louis, Mo: Washington University, 1964 (p. 6)

54　W. Blaser *Mies van der Rohe* London: Thames and Hudson, 1972 (p. 49)

55　"Interview with Aldo Rossi" *Japan Architect* no. 1, 1985 (p. 12)

56　D. Libeskind "Deconstruction of Architecture" *Lotus* no. 32, 1981 (p. 94)

57　Gaudet, op cit

58　Umberto Eco, quoted by Anthony Burgess in "Reflections on the *Name of the Rose*" *South China Morning Post* April 1985. Verbatim: "A novel Eco says, is 'a machine for generating interpretations,' and the novelist should not load the dice in favour of one interpretation rather than another."

Figure credits

14　R. Pricke *The Ornaments of Architecture* London, 1674

15　*Architectural Design and Construction Manual of the Sung Dynasty* new edition (in Chinese), Architect Asia Publishing Ltd, Hong Kong, 1983

16F　E. & C. Neuenschwander *Alvar Aalto and Finnish Architecture* London: Architectural Press, 1954 (p. 155)

17　Sebastiano Serlio *Tutte l'opera d'architectura* 1584

18　W.R. Ware *The American Vignola* republished by Norton, New York, 1977

19　J. Ruskin *The Stones of Venice*

25,26 daVinci software by Hayden Software Company, Lowell, Mass

33　The Soane Museum, London

34　Vicenzo Scamozzi *L'Idea della architettura universale* Venice, 1615

35,36,37 Durand *Precis* and *Partie graphique*

38　G. Stiny & W. Mitchell "Counting Palladian plans" *Environment & Planning B* vol. 5, 1978 (pp. 189-198)

45　Durand, op cit

46　J. Guiton *The Ideas of Le Corbusier* New York: Braziller, 1981 (p. 28)

56　C. Rowe, R. Slutzky & B. Hoesli *Transparenz* Basel: Birkhauser, 1968

57　P. Carter *Mies van der Robe at Work* London: Pall Mall, 1974 (p. 87)

58　C. Rowe *The Mathematics of the Ideal Villa and Other Essays* (p. 5)

All other illustrations are by the authors or students at Hong Kong University.